Brave Bessie

Flying Free

by

Lillian M. Fisher

 Hendrick-Long Publishing Co.

Dallas, Texas 75225

Library of Congress Cataloging-in-Publication Data
Fisher, Lillian M.
    Brave Bessie : flying free / Lillian M. Fisher.
        p. cm.
    Includes bibliographical references and index.
    ISBN 0-937460-94-X (hardcover)
        1. Coleman, Bessie, 1896-1926. 2. Afro-American air pilots—
United States—Biography. 3. Women air pilots—United States—
Biography. I. Title. TL540.C646F57 1995
629.13'092—dc2O
[B]   95-8546
                                                                          CIP

Design and Production
Intentions Graphic Design (Dallas, Texas)

10 9 8 7 6 5 4 3 2 1

 Hendrick-Long Publishing Co.

P.O. Box 25123
Dallas, Texas 75225-1123

Brave Bessie

Flying Free

Bessie's Song

I climb, I soar

Higher, high

Above the cotton

Fields I fly.

Unleashed,

Unbound,

My spirit free

Beyond the clouds

On wings I flee

Alone with wind,

Sweet air, and sun

I sing the song

Of battles won.

My plane arrests

An icy blast.

And on into the sun

I'm free at last!

Lillian M. Fisher

For my husband, Robert

Chapter 1

$\mathcal{B}$essie strode onto the field looking as if she owned it, her back straight, head erect. The crowd cheered wildly as Bessie smiled and waved. Her small figure, dressed neatly in a military type uniform, complete with puttees, shirt, jacket, a wide Sam Browne belt, and high boots, gave the impression of importance. Slowly turning her head in all directions, she smiled again, took off her hat, and waved it in the air. Her short black hair blew freely in the wind.

The sun shone on that Labor Day weekend in 1922 at Curtiss Field on Long Island, New York. The viewing stands came alive with the noisy excited mass of eager people waiting to see Bessie's first air show. Bessie loved to fly and was anxious to show off her skills. She would give the people her best, give them their money's worth. In turn she would be paid very well for performing daring acts in the sky.

Unlike air travel today, which is safe, flying planes in 1922 could be dangerous, and too often pilots who flew stunts—upside down, in loops, and low to the ground—crashed.

This day, Bessie's day, the Curtiss's propeller had been wound for take off. It whirred so fast it couldn't be seen. Bessie took off her hat and handed it to her helper. She put on a helmet and goggles and climbed into the waiting plane, still waving. The crowd cheered even louder now.

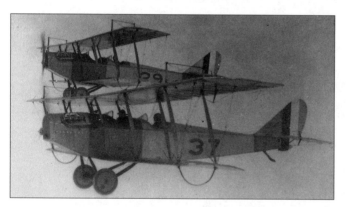

Curtiss JN-4s, or "Jennys"

To Bessie, the plane looked like a beautiful butterfly made of struts and wires, canvas and glue. The Curtiss, also called "Jenny" and named for Glenn Curtiss, a leader among airplane builders, was the first successful mass-produced airplane used in business. This aircraft introduced America to flying.

Bessie took a deep breath, pulled gently on the control stick (joystick) and taxied down the runway, slowly picking up speed. The plane bumped along for a while and then suddenly, as if by magic, it lifted and soared gracefully into the sky.

The wind whipped Bessie's face, icy cold air so strong it forced her back against the seat. The flying wires whistled, and Bessie laughed for joy, her white silk scarf streaming behind her. From the open cockpit she looked down. The field below shrank to a tiny square. Trees became the size of bushes, and houses seemed like small blocks. The engine churned, and she soared upward. Now Bessie teased the crowd. She flew upside down and with a wide sweep she brought the plane back. She swooped down as if to nose dive, then up again. She and the Curtiss went through the stunts perfectly. This was Bessie's show, and she performed as a star!

Bessie Coleman, in 1921, became the first black female licensed pilot in the world. This was especially remarkable because when aviation first began, women did not get encouragement to fly planes. In a field dominated by men, women who wanted to fly did not have much of a chance. Think how nearly impossible it must have been for Bessie, part Indian, part black, and a female. She had to overcome almost overwhelming barriers of poverty and prejudice in order to realize her goal and take to the skies.

Bessie was born on January 26, 1893, in Atlanta, Texas, near the Arkansas state line. She later lived in Waxahachie, a small farming community thirty miles south of Dallas. It would be ten years before Wilbur and

Orville Wright would build the first flying machine.

The Coleman family, who had almost no money, moved to Oklahoma when Bessie was a baby. Oklahoma Territory had been home to the Cherokee Nation since 1838. George

Coleman, Bessie's father, three-fourths Cherokee Indian, wanted to live with his people. Her mother, Susan Coleman, an African American, wanted to move back to Texas. The family returned to Texas to the little town called Waxahachie. But Bessie's father longed to live with the Cherokees, one of the most important of the Five Civilized Tribes. Bessie, a seven-year-old, loved her father and wanted him to stay in Texas, but he decided that he belonged in Oklahoma, and he returned to the reservation.

Susan Coleman, stubborn and strong willed, refused to move her family back to Oklahoma. Only nine of her thirteen children had lived. By now, five of the eldest had left home and only Bessie, Elois, Nilus, and Georgia remained. Mrs. Coleman worked very hard and managed to support her children by taking in washing. She also ironed clothes for the people in Waxahachie, working from early morning to late at night.

Bessie saw that her mother's life was hard, and she wanted to help. As soon as she was about eight, she and Elois picked cotton for neighboring farmers and brought home money. They helped their mother with the laundry and the ironing.

Nilus and Georgia, Bessie's two younger sisters, were still too small to help much.

Mr. and Mrs. Coleman had built the small three-room home themselves and furnished it with a few chairs, a table, beds, and a stove. The house had no plumbing or running water. Mrs. Coleman did her laundry outside in a big tub. Bent over the washboard, she scrubbed the clothes so hard it hurt her back. The family washed and bathed on the porch in all kinds of weather. An outhouse nestled in a grove of honeysuckle behind the house.

Bessie helped her mother plant a garden each year. She found it wonderful to see sprouts of beans, sweet corn, and even peanuts come out of the ground every spring. Bessie and her sisters weeded, watered, and helped care for the garden. A small orchard beyond the cabin provided apples, peaches, and pears. Bessie loved flowers as much as her mother did and planted them all around the house. Honeysuckle thrived, as well as sweet smelling roses, lilacs, and other flowers.

Susan Coleman could not read or write, but she wanted

an education for her children. Black and poor white children attended school whenever they could because they had to work to help their parents harvest crops or pick cotton.

Mrs. Coleman managed to borrow books from a book wagon that came to the small town now and then. Bessie and Elois attended a poor black school when they could, but since the teachers were usually untrained and unpaid, the kind of education they offered was not very good.

Bessie kept the business records for her mother. She carefully entered an accounting of the family's meager earnings and expenses in

Ten thousand bales of cotton waiting for shipment from Waxahachie, Texas, early 1900s

a ledger. She was good at arithmetic and could add and subtract, multiply and divide.

When Bessie was very young she hungered for learning. She longed to go to a full-time school. But while other children went to school, she and Elois often went into the fields to pick cotton. Bessie knew that getting an education was the only way she could rise above the hard life she lived and often said, "We have to get above these cotton fields." Perhaps the desire to live better gave her the motivation she needed to later pursue a flying career.

Bessie wanted more than anything to learn to read. The books her mother borrowed made her want to learn more. She studied them for hours, matching words to the pictures. She already knew the alphabet. After much trial and error she tapped the secret code of the letters and taught herself to read. Her belief that education was the only way to rise above her present condition, together with her

An advertisement for Uncle Tom's Cabin

mother's constant faith and encouragement, made her determined to succeed.

Once Bessie could read, she read about the lives of Harriet Tubman, Booker T. Washington, and many other famous African Americans. Reading about these wonderful people, her people, strengthened a belief in herself. She decided that if these important blacks could overcome countless hardships and accomplish wonderful things, then so could she. When Bessie read *Uncle Tom's Cabin*, the story brought tears to her eyes. She said, "I'll never be a Topsy or an Uncle Tom." Early in Bessie's life she made a promise to help herself, as well as her family and her race.

Now that Bessie could read, she read the Bible to her family every evening. Susan Coleman was very religious and saw to it that her children went to the Missionary Baptist Church regularly. Bessie, baptized at the age of twelve, attended Sunday School and learned about God. At Sunday School she practiced reading and spelling, and she discovered history.

Bessie loved Sundays. Her time spent at church gave her a strong faith in God, and the knowledge that hard work, patience, and courage would get her through the hardest times.

She loved the singing, listened to the sermons and enjoyed the peace of the church filled with people she knew, friends and neighbors. Ladies fanned themselves with little cardboard fans, advertising items from stores, and even funeral parlors. People, dressed in their Sunday best, enjoyed lemonade and cookies after the service.

One Sunday the pastor announced that the church planned a fund-raising raffle. In order to excite members to sell tickets for the event, he offered a contest. Whoever sold the most tickets would win a prize. Bessie wanted that prize, a beautiful hand organ. Whatever she did, she had determination to do the best that she knew how. She sold tickets, sold more than anyone, and won the hand organ! That was Bessie, always going the extra mile, pushing herself a little harder, always aiming to do her best.

Chapter 2

$\mathcal{E}$very year, sometimes until late December, Bessie and Elois trudged down the path to the cotton fields early each morning. It seemed to Bessie it was always cotton picking time. One day, as she looked out beyond the fields, white like snow as far as the eye could see, the sky filled with puffy white clouds. They appeared to come down and touch the earth. A flock of birds flew in V formation against the sky and as Bessie watched them soar and disappear she wished with all her heart that she could fly like that. Then she'd get above the cotton fields.

This year, December brought unusually warm weather and the cotton harvest seemed to go on forever. But Christmas, so close now, made everything feel a bit magical. Mrs.

Coleman had saved a part of her earnings to give the girls a fine Christmas, and the day before the holiday the cotton harvest finally ended. Bessie and Elois ran all the way home. They could hardly wait to give their mother the new scarf they bought at Mr. Wilson's General Store with pennies they had saved.

Mrs. Coleman, by the light of a kerosene lamp, had worked many nights after Nilus and Georgia had gone to bed. She made rag dolls and fashioned clothes from flour sacks. She had bought a small tin toy for each of them, a gray striped cat with a ball between its paws for Nilus and a brown tin dog with a tail for Georgia. The toys had keys and when the animals were wound the cat crawled and the dog wagged its tail. She bought Bessie a new book. A good customer had given Mrs. Coleman a stack of magazines and these, too, were for Bessie. A new pair of shoes wrapped in Christmas paper were set aside for Elois, along with bright red ribbons for her hair.

The big white hen, too old now to lay eggs, had been killed, plucked, and cleaned, and on Christmas morning it roasted in a blue enamel pan in the oven of the wood cook stove. Black-eyed peas, corn bread, mashed potatoes, and greens completed the feast. Bessie thought this was the most wonderful Christmas she had ever had. But she missed her father and wished he could be there to celebrate Christmas with them. Maybe some day, she thought, he would come home.

The books and the magazines excited Bessie. One of the magazines, called the *Delineator*, printed wonderful stories. Another magazine printed an article about the Wright brothers and their latest wonderful flying machine. Bessie thrilled when she saw the picture of the plane, a two-seat military Flyer with a set of wings, one on top of the plane and one underneath. The plane had a completely open cockpit and the pilot and passenger sat in a wooden frame without any protection from the weather. Bessie closed her eyes and tried to imagine what it would be like to be up in the clouds and rule the sky.

Bessie wanted to know more about flying. She asked the lady who brought books to town in a wagon to please bring books about airplanes and pilots. Bessie could hardly wait for the next time the wagon came, but come it did, and there were books about airplanes for Bessie!

Bessie read by the kerosene lamp every evening. She studied the books and pictures. She made crude sketches of the flying machines and drew her own models. Every now and then a plane flew over Waxahachie. Bessie knew the engine's sound well, and even before the plane appeared overhead, she rushed outside, shielded her eyes, and watched for the great mechanical bird. When it came closer she jumped up and down and waved wildly. Maybe the pilot saw her and maybe he didn't. But that didn't seem to matter to Bessie. She needed to call out, signal the pilot, shout to him that she would be up there someday. The sky would be hers, too. She would be free!

But life in the cabin wasn't all drudgery. In spite of hard work Bessie and her sisters had good times, too. The circus came to town every spring. Mrs. Coleman gave Bessie and Elois a fifty cent piece to spend any way they wished. They took along a pail of food from home, corn bread and fruit, to make their money go further. They bought cotton candy, pink lemonade, and balloons. They rode the merry-go-round and enjoyed the side shows.

In 1914, World War I was declared, but the United States did not join the fight until April 6, 1917. Women enrolled in the Red Cross, studied nursing, made bandages and tried in every way to help the war effort. Now more and more stories about airplanes appeared in newspapers and magazines, and Bessie read everything she could get her hands on.

At the start of the war, the fighter plane had not been created by American design. When America entered the fight, her allies used only French and British flying machines. But suddenly Americans began to experiment with their own airplane models. It amazed Bessie that in four short years the plane changed from a flimsy aircraft, one that looked like a crate with linen wings, into a sturdy looking plane. New designs followed one right after the other, each new plane an improvement over the one that came before.

In the United States, Tommy Sopwith formed his own company and manufactured the Bat Boat, a plane made of a wooden body, canvas wings, and wires. The pilot now sat inside a cockpit and could speed to ninety-two and a half

miles an hour and climb
at the rate of 1,200 feet
per minute. Tommy
became the first to
invent the triplane, a
craft with three wings.

Sopwith Camel

The British had their
Pups, Camels, and SE5As. The Pup, a Sopwith design, simple
and lightweight, had a fire resistant engine bulkhead.
Aluminum protected the wood on this part of the plane, the
bulkhead or main
section, and linen
covered the rest.
The designers used
spruce to make the
wing spars and
ribs, and metal
tubes covered with

Fokker Triplane

cloth formed the tips of the wings. A single machine gun was
mounted on the fuselage. The craft had an 80-horsepower
engine and the entire plane weighed 800 pounds.

Anthony Fokker, a Dutchman, designed a number of fighting planes for Germany. Manfred Von Richthofen, a great ace of World War I known as the Red Baron, flew a blood red Fokker Triplane. He killed many air soldiers and his countrymen viewed him as a hero.

SPAD VII

The French had their SPAD, a plane that steadily improved until the final SPAD could do 130 miles an hour and climb to 22,000 feet. Like other planes of its day, it was made of wood with a wire-braced fuselage, hollow box section spars and wing ribs made of spruce, and wire bracings.

Bessie studied and loved these planes, the planes she was determined to fly. When she told her mother about her desire to become a pilot, her mother did not encourage her. Mrs. Coleman had the opinion that there were other professions less risky and more in keeping with what women could expect to do, such as teaching or clerking. Mrs. Coleman, every bit as determined as Bessie, realized that Bessie *had* to get an education.

One of the most exciting days in Bessie's life was the time her mother came home with wonderful news that Bessie could go to school full time. Although Bessie had often dreamed of getting an education, she always feared her chances of realizing that goal were slim. Schooling was the only way she'd ever "get above the cotton fields." To attend school full time became Bessie's opportunity. She would give it her best!

On a Monday morning Bessie wore her starched blue dress and tied her braids with strips of new cloth. Mrs. Coleman, with tears in her eyes, hugged Bessie hard. Her Bessie was going to be *somebody*.

The black school had good teachers and Bessie learned quickly. She already had a good grasp of many subjects. She had fun learning other things as well. Bessie learned a popular song of the day, "Come Josephine In My Flying Machine,"* written by Alfred Bryan and inspired by the excitement and awe of the airplane.

Bessie did very well in all her subjects. She passed her

See page 81.

exams and graduated. Mrs. Coleman, Elois, Nilus, and Georgia dressed in their best clothes and went to see Bessie graduate. Mrs. Coleman wore a black hat one of her customers had given her. She sewed new ribbons on it and it looked nice. Elois, Nilus, and Georgia wore made-overs, and Bessie thought they looked so good no one would ever know the clothes had been remade.

On a sultry Friday afternoon in 1910, the school auditorium was stuffy and crowded. Mrs. Coleman sat with her children around her. When Bessie's name was called, the little family stood up and clapped loudly. They were so proud of Bessie.

Mrs. Coleman had always been thrifty. She saved a portion of her small earnings every week, along with some money her children brought home. She kept this money she called her "nest egg" in a big glass fruit jar on the top shelf of the cupboard. In the evening, after Bessie's graduation ceremony, Mrs. Coleman took the jar from the cupboard and spread the money out on the faded oilcloth that served as a table cover. It looked like a lot of money to Bessie and her sisters. It was enough to see Bessie through one year at

Langston Industrial College, now Langston University. If students could pass entrance exams, they could attend college.

The school, 400 miles north of Waxahachie, was located in the rolling hills of central Oklahoma. Many years later Bessie's niece and nephew attended that school.

Bessie had never been away from her family. She missed them, but her studies kept her busy. She spent much of her free time in the library, learning more about airplanes and flying. For as long as she could remember she knew in her heart that someday she would become a pilot. She thought about flying constantly, knowing the only way to reach that goal was through more

Waxahachie, about 1916

education.

To Bessie's dismay, her money ran out after one semester, even though she had been careful how she spent every penny. Heartbroken at having to leave college, she came home determined to find a job that would provide enough money for more schooling. But Waxahachie had few jobs that paid well, and none for Bessie. She took in washing, did housework, minded white children, and picked cotton. Bessie wanted more and so did her mother. Mrs. Coleman had the answer. She wanted Bessie to go to Chicago and stay with her brothers, Walter and John, and find work there.

One morning in 1915 when gray clouds hung low to the earth and a cold wind blew from the north, Mrs. Coleman, Nilus, Georgia, and Elois, walked with Bessie to the train station in Waxahachie. With tears streaming down her cheeks, Bessie hugged her mother and sisters in turn, and boarded the train for the trip to Chicago. She was forced to sit in the last car, the one reserved for blacks. She waved to her family from the window of the train and smiled. Bessie was optimistic as ever.

Chapter 3

The soot from the train's smokestack covered everything with grime, including Bessie. Her white blouse became soiled with soot, and the artificial cherries on her straw hat drooped. She had been seated by the murky window for two whole days while the big steam engine swayed in rough rhythm, stopping now and then at depots to let some people off and to let new passengers board. Bessie dozed as the noise of the wheels on the track, the clickety-clack, clickety-clack, pounded in her ears. Her stomach growled. The sandwiches her mother had packed ran out the first day, and she felt hungry.

The giant noisy monster came to a grinding halt, and Bessie roused from her dreaming. She looked out the window at a sight she would always remember. She had never seen so many people, people in a hurry, scurrying about in all directions. She saw snow falling and men, women, and children, bundled in warm coats, scarves, gloves and boots. People held on to their hats because the strong wind could carry them away. This had to be Chicago, the Windy City, Bessie thought. Then the conductor called out, "Now boarding . . . now unloading. Chicago, Illinois!"

Suddenly Bessie found herself standing on a platform with noise and bustle all around. Car engines put-putted in the streets, horns honked, and drivers moved their cars rapidly everywhere she looked. Many of the cars, Model T Fords called "Tin Lizzies," had been made by Henry Ford, who said the cars would come in any color as long as that color was black. Bessie had seen a few automobiles in Waxahachie, but in that small town mostly horses pulled wagons.

All the noise and commotion of the big city excited Bessie. She looked up at the skyscrapers, buildings that seemed to touch the clouds. They were so high she worried that airplanes might get tangled up in them. Bessie fell in love with Chicago, with the action, the sights, the sounds.

She wouldn't have a chance to become homesick.

She heard someone call, "Bessie? Bessie!" and she turned and threw her arms around her brothers, Walter and John. They laughed and talked all at once. There was so much to talk about. John and Walter wanted to hear news of Mama and the girls. Bessie, curious about Chicago, had many questions she wanted answered.

John's apartment, a cold-water flat, perched on the second floor of a shabby house. A cold-water flat had plumbing and running water, but no hot water. That didn't pose much of a problem. Water could be heated on the stove in kettles, even enough for baths. Steam heat warmed the dwelling, and radiators in every room hissed and banged, as they kept the apartment warm.

The very next day after Bessie's arrival she went looking for work. She read the newspaper want ads and checked off jobs she thought she could fill. She left the apartment early, hoping to be the first one to apply for a clerk's job. The winter cold forced her to draw her coat tighter. She held on to her hat and walked down the slippery sidewalk coated with a thin sheet of ice.

As Bessie walked in the city streets, she smelled a sicken-
ingly sweet, smoky odor that wafted from the packing houses.
Chimneys belched their black smoke, factories poured out
steam and smog, and wonderful airplanes flew the skies. Not
just one machine, but many kinds of aircraft traveled back
and forth in the skies. Bessie caught her breath. The sound of
the engines was like music to her ears. Standing on the sidewalk, gaping at the sky, Bessie promised herself, as she had
many times, she would learn to fly. Soon!

A grand parade of women, dressed in white, marched
toward her; rows of women filled the street. The women in
the lead struggled to steady a banner against the strong wind.
Bessie read the message as it floated past. "Women have a
right to vote!" The words made Bessie's whole being tingle.
How wonderful it would be, she thought, if women were
allowed to vote!

Bessie smiled at the women. They called themselves suffragettes. She admired anyone who tried to change whatever
was unfair. One woman smiled back at Bessie. Bessie felt a
kinship toward the woman, feelings she had for a sister. Not
until 1920 with the passage of the Nineteenth Amendment

to the United States Constitution would women be allowed to vote. Black men had been given the right to vote in 1870, but women still could not vote.

Bessie applied for many jobs, but no one would hire her. One man laughed and said, "You oughta know better. We don't hire Negroes here." Others shook their heads or quickly said, "No!" But Bessie didn't get discouraged easily. She decided she would just keep trying.

John and Walter loved their sister and worried about her. They knew it would be hard for Bessie to find a job, but they reasoned that if she trained for a special occupation she would have an easier time of it. They loaned Bessie enough money to enroll in a beauty culture school.

Bessie studied hard, observed, listened, and learned the cosmetic trade quickly. As always, she put forth extra effort and passed the course faster than her classmates. She went to work as a manicurist in the White Sox Barber Shop. The shop, owned by the trainer of Chicago's American League baseball club, paid Bessie well. It wasn't long before she was able to repay Walter and John. Now she could think seriously about taking flying lessons!

One day a small black boy brought an airplane into the barbershop to show Bessie. She was delighted with the model and displayed it in the window of the shop. She loved planes, any kind, giant airships or toy models. Bessie told the boy about her plans to fly. He became just as excited as Bessie.

Bessie applied to one flying school after another. The answer always came back the same. No! She said, "I was Indian, I was Negro, I was female. And I wanted to fly." It proved to be harder for Bessie than for white women applying to flying schools. Many white women were denied admission because of their sex. Bessie had an additional handicap. She was also a woman of color.

Robert Sengstacke Abbott, publisher of the *Chicago Defender*, a newspaper, often came to the barbershop where Bessie worked. While Bessie manicured his nails, they talked of many things. Mr. Abbott's newspaper liked crusades to help people, and he enjoyed printing articles about subjects that excited people, even shocked them. Bessie enjoyed listening to Mr. Abbott, and he came to know her better. He soon discovered Bessie's interest in aviation. She fascinated him. Imagine! A black woman determined to become a pilot!

When Bessie told Mr. Abbott about the many American flying schools that had turned her down, and how much she wanted to fly, he took a deep interest in her dream. He decided to help her. He kept in touch with a mass of information and knew many people. He asked a lot of his friends about flying schools for Bessie. He knew that American air schools would never admit her, so he investigated European schools and came up with a solution.

Mr. Abbott told Bessie that if she wanted flying lessons, she would have to travel to Europe to get them. France, he said, governed parts of Africa and educated many Africans in Paris. French people found Africans exotic. Paris, in particular, during the postwar period, welcomed creative people, and Parisians acted open and friendly to outsiders. Among some of the famous Americans who flocked to Paris after the war were writers F. Scott Fitzgerald and Ernest Hemingway.

In America, while the law said blacks were free, they were still denied the good living white people enjoyed. France had a more tolerant attitude toward all people, so Mr. Abbott told Bessie that France was the perfect place for her to learn to fly. Many good flying schools were located there.

Bessie was excited. She had the money for her lessons, and she became eager to sail for France. First, she had to enroll in a night school class and learn the French language. Mr. Abbott said she would be expected to converse with people who might not speak English.

French lessons did not appear to be difficult for Bessie. After a few months she had learned enough French, and she decided to leave for Europe.

When John and Walter heard of Bessie's plans, they did not encourage her. Flying was dangerous, and they believed their sister was putting her life at risk. Bessie's mother, again, worried about her daughter's safety and tried to change Bessie's mind. But Bessie, as always, said that nothing could stop her. She wanted to become a flyer and fly the skies. Then she would be free! She believed that the money she had saved would carry her through her training period; she made all the necessary plans for her trip to France.

Chapter 4

In 1920, Woodrow Wilson was the president of the United States. Movies, called *picture shows*, did not have sound yet, and showed only pictures. Mary Pickford, a leading Hollywood starlet, enjoyed the name "America's Sweetheart." Radio began its first regular broadcasts, though not many people owned radio sets.

In November of 1920, Bessie sailed for Paris with a Red Cross Unit. The long voyage at sea gave her much time to study. Sometimes she sat on the deck and watched for planes. She saw some birds and fewer planes, but once she got to France so many planes filled the sky it seemed as if they were part of the universe, like the sun, the moon, and the stars.

First, Bessie went to Avord, France, a small village with

cobblestone walks and winding roads, centered in a flat green countryside dotted with farmhouses and trees. An enormous flying school was located nearby. It seemed to Bessie that aerodromes stretched for miles, along with countless hangars, hundreds of men . . . and some women. Men and women who wanted to fly!

The first French school to which she applied rejected her. Not because of her race, but because the school had lost students the week before in fatal crashes. Flying was dangerous, not just for women, but for men as well. Bessie did find a school in Le Crotoy. She stayed at a farm house and walked to the flying school.

The farmer's wife served *beaucoup bon* (coffee) and chocolate, and a bottle of *vin ordinaire* (wine) at every meal. Bessie especially liked the omelets, goat cheese, and strawberry tarts.

During the first few weeks at Le Crotoy, students had lessons taught in the classroom. They learned about the special parts of the airplane and their purposes. Bessie was so excited she could hardly speak when her instructor announced that on the following Monday she would train in a penguin. Penguins were like little grass-cutters and looked like planes without wings. Bessie ran them in a straight line back and forth on the field. Some of the students crashed, but Bessie broke not a wire.

Then came the next step, the roller. The roller, a small plane, actually had wings! It could fly, but the instructor cautioned Bessie not to try. She and the other students ran the rollers in straight lines, just like the penguins, getting ready for the next step, flying, in a real *airplane* up in the sky!

Now Bessie would become a pilot, just as soon as she completed the required hours of flying. Many of the students used the monoplane that had one main supporting wing. The biplane had two wings, one directly above the other, but the triplane, an airplane with three supporting wings, seemed to be the plane most students loved best. Bessie favored that one, too.

Bessie could hardly wait to find out which type of plane her instructor would choose for her to make a solo flight. The last stage of training was called *Tour de Piste*. The night before her first flight the excitement of realizing her goal robbed her of sleep, and she couldn't eat a bite even though the farmer's wife cautioned that if Bessie wanted to fly well she must eat!

Clouds hung over the flying fields in the morning like a thick blanket. Bessie, dressed in a brown leather jacket, scarf, jodhpurs, helmet and goggles, waited impatiently for the weather to clear. She paced back and forth, watching the sky. By noon the clouds parted and the sun shone through.

Bessie's heart beat faster as the mechanic brought the plane onto the runway. The machine assigned to Bessie had flown the skies in World War I. Its shabby linen wings reminded her of a late season dragonfly that had seen too many suns, too much wind and rain. There was one difference. Giant bull's eyes had been painted on the undersides of the wings, blue and white circles with a red center. The plane looked wonderful to Bessie.

After the wood propeller had been wound, the mechanic dodged out of the way. The cylinders began firing, and Bessie taxied down the field and turned the tail to the wind. The plane bumped along to the end of the field. Bessie pulled gently on the joystick. Up, up she went. The plane left the ground, and Bessie flew into the sky.

She moved high above the clouds, the cold wind hard against her face, almost taking her breath away. The wing

Bessie Coleman's pilot license, June 15, 1921

wires sang, the motor purred, and Bessie was free! "I did it," she said. "I got above those cotton fields!"

For the next six months Bessie studied and flew. She hired only the best instructors, including the chief pilot for Anthony Fokker's Aircraft Company. The Fokker company was one of the leading aircraft makers in the world. Anthony Fokker had supplied planes for Germany in World War I. After the war he set up companies in America.

Photograph used on the license

On June 15, 1921, she received her pilot's license. She became the first

40

licensed black woman pilot in the world! Now she held the key to success. Her license would open skies to her. Europeans loved her. She would make Americans love her, too. But Bessie wasn't satisfied with ordinary flying. She was determined to get additional training, training that would teach her to perform stunts and aerobatics. However, that kind of training would take money, and Bessie's money ran out.

Bessie returned to the United States on September 16, 1921, in good spirits and settled again in Chicago. She was deter-mined to earn enough money to go back to France for special training. She opened a chili parlor. If Bessie could cook anything well, it was good Texas chili. Bessie's busi-ness turned out to be a great success. In her thrifty manner she saved her profits, and on February 22, 1922, she returned to France, this time with plenty of cash.

Bessie's mother, Susan Coleman, with a silver cup given to Bessie in New York, 1921, by the cast of Shuffle Along, *an all-black musical*

Bessie's teachers taught her difficult and dangerous air maneuvers. All of her instructors believed she had natural piloting ability. Often some of her fellow students cracked up, and some died. Every time it happened, Bessie wiped the tears from her eyes, got back into the cockpit, and flew again. A flyer had to have courage. A flyer had to love flying more than anything else in the world.

Bessie took to the air as if born to fly. At Staaken, the flying field on the outskirts of Berlin, she flew a 2,200-horsepower Benz motored L.F.G. plane without any instruction at all. She became the first woman to pilot this two-seater airplane, much to the amazement of even veteran pilots. Bessie became a hit in European air society. She was on her way!

Chapter 5

$\mathcal{I}$n August, 1922, Bessie booked passage on the American liner SS *Noordam* and sailed for home. The *New York Times* published an article on August 14 about Bessie. The headline read: NEGRO AVIATRIX ARRIVES. "Termed by leading French and Dutch aviators one of the best flyers they had seen, Miss Bessie Coleman, said to be the only negro aviatrix in the world, returned from Europe yesterday to give a series of exhibitions in this country, particularly among her own people. . . ."

Walter and John, though proud of Bessie, continued to worry about her flying. Aviation was dangerous. Nevertheless, Bessie announced, in her determined way, that she planned to perform in her first air show in New York at

Curtiss Field on Labor Day weekend.

The crowd on that memorable day went wild when they saw Bessie walk onto the field. They waved, whistled, yelled, and threw their hats in the air. Flyers were heroes, but women flyers were something more. And a black woman pilot. . . . Wow! ·

Bessie loved to show off. Sitting in the open cockpit of the Curtiss, first she did an Immelmann, a half-roll on top of a half-loop, then loop-the-loops, figure eights, and a Richthofen glide, the maneuver named for the Red Baron. She cut the engine and went into a wonderful glide before pulling up and doing barrel rolls. People loved it.

About a month later, Bessie performed at Chicago's Checkerboard Aerodrome. Today it is known as Midway Airport. The Chicago Defender advertised Bessie as a coming attraction. Mr. Abbott was proud of Bessie, too.

Bessie was blessed with good showmanship, and she wanted to make this a memorable show; something wonderful— something people would never forget. She brought her sister, Georgia, to Chicago, hoping to make her sister part of the spectacular show. Bessie hired a dressmaker to make a suit of red, white, and blue fabric, shiny silk with bangles all over. She wanted Georgia to make a parachute jump but thought she'd wait until the very last minute to tell her sister. That way Georgia couldn't say no. When the day of the big show arrived and Bessie told Georgia about the parachute jump, Georgia looked Bessie in the eyes and said, "Huh, uh, not me!"

Even without Georgia the show was a fantastic success. Bessie flew her plane high, doing her stunts, breathtaking moves that excited the crowd and filled Bessie with joy. Then, during one of the stunts, Bessie's engine began to sputter. The engine died. To the people on the ground it looked as if she'd lost control. The Curtiss, moving fast, nose dived to earth. Again the engine coughed and sputtered. Even Bessie thought she was going to crash. Suddenly the engine began to churn evenly. Bessie regained control of the plane, thanked God, and flew gracefully into the sun, circled the field, and landed smoothly. Her performance at this event earned her not only the love and respect of the audience, but a new name, *Brave Bessie*.

Bessie enjoyed the success of many air shows after that.

When she read about barnstorming and watched some of that dangerous flying, she decided she had to become a barnstormer.

Barnstormers roamed the country and rented cow pastures where they put on their air shows. First the flyer would fly a test to see if a good crowd would show up. The pilot would zoom in, circle the field, wait and watch. When people gathered, the flyer would land, ask to rent the farmer's field and charge admission. Sometimes a ten-minute ride in the air cost as much as $4. The farmer got a free ride.

The barnstormers called themselves "gypsies," and flew low, zoomed high above the barns, and sometimes flew *through* the open barns. These air stunt pilots did loop-the-loops, figure eights, even flew upside down.

Bessie made up her mind to be a barnstormer because she wanted to try something more daring than regular stunt flying. Barnstorming was very dangerous, but popular, and it paid well. Bessie went back to Houston, Texas, and began her new barnstorming career.

More and more now the public clamored for daring air shows, and all over the country air acrobatics were in demand. Bessie delighted in being an unusual attraction. A black female pilot, unheard of until now, drew crowds of curious people. In the past, Bessie's race had been a handicap. Now it became the very reason people flocked to see her perform.

Bessie preferred the Curtiss plane, the "Jenny" named for the JN-4D. Its bee-like hum droned above the cow pastures, and the plane landed like magic. She always waited for the crowd to show, and dozens of spectators always came. People lined up to ride in her plane even for five minutes. She wore leather and goggles and fed the machine oil and gasoline from battered cans.

Barnstorming was not all flying. Bessie spent hours on the ground repairing her plane when things went wrong. Often the fragile wings needed mending. Fabric covered the wood spars and ribs, and often these needed doping. The dope was a kind of glue. Spark plugs required regular cleaning, and the planes were always thirsty for *sauce* (gasoline). Often Bessie walked to the local gas station, five or more miles away, to get a refill of gasoline to start her plane. Still, the money she earned was more than she had ever expected, and flying never seemed like work.

About the time of Bessie's barnstorming career, Charles A. Lindbergh, who in 1927 became famous for his nonstop flight from America to Paris, began his flying career. He, too, went into the barnstorming business. During this same period, the equally famous Amelia Earhart followed in

Barnstorming

Bessie's and Lindbergh's footsteps. This fledgling flyer would one day become world famous.

Wing walkers performed one of the most dangerous of all stunts in those barnstorming days. Wing walkers, men and women, actually walked on the wings of planes as they soared high in the sky. Sometimes rope ladders, suspended from the undersides of planes, allowed the wing walkers to transfer

Barnstorming

from one aircraft to another. Many walkers fell to their deaths, but people thronged to the air fields to view the daring performers.

Bessie, always an important flyer in these air shows, invented her own flying style. She zoomed over the field, flying as low as she could, aiming for the roof of the barn. Everyone just knew she would crash. When it looked as if Bessie might crack up, she would suddenly force the plane up and up, gliding gracefully, flying figure eights, loop-the-loops, and turning upside down. The crowds screamed. "More! More!"

Bessie knew the air fields and flying schools in Texas. One of the schools she visited in Houston, where she spent much of her flying time, had been opened by the mother of Katherine Stinson, a veteran aviatrix.

Bessie remembered well the difficult time she had trying to gain admission to American flying schools. She remembered the humiliation, her disappointment, her anger. She didn't want this to happen to her people any longer. As she thought about this problem, a wonderful idea began to take shape in her mind, and, the more she thought about it, the more she convinced herself that *she*, in some way, must change conditions for people like herself.

She decided to open a flying school for people of color! Since Bessie was very young she had wanted to help her people advance. If she opened a flying school she would help make it easier for blacks to become flyers.

Chapter 6

Waxahachie, two hundred miles from Houston, was a short distance by air. Bessie, anxious to visit her mother, flew to the small town where she grew up.

The reunion with her mother was wonderful. What had always been a close relationship had not suffered from separation. Susan Coleman, proud of her daughter's accomplishments, still feared for her safety. Again, she tried to discourage Bessie from continuing her flying.

As they had done in the past, they sat by the light of the kerosene lamp and talked of many things. Bessie tried to make her mother realize that flying was the only thing she wanted to do. Regardless of the dangers, it was something she had to do. She said, "If I can create the minimum of my plans and desires, there shall be no regrets." Bessie was in love with flying.

The sleepy little town of Waxahachie had grown. It now had a college with grounds around it. Bessie was asked to fly her plane in an air show, and she wanted to show off her skills to the hometown folk.

The weather, beautiful sunny Texas weather, greeted the day. As Bessie came onto the field the morning of the air show, she noticed two entrances, one for whites, and one for blacks.

Bessie marched into the main building and went to the office, sadness in her heart and anger on her lips. To the manager's surprise, Bessie demanded that her people be allowed to come onto the field through the same gate as whites, and she said if this was not allowed she would not perform.

Bessie got her wish, and she performed that day, carrying on a spectacular show for all. When the show ended, Bessie noticed that her people had been separated after being admitted. Two viewing sections had been roped off, one for whites and one for blacks.

Bessie planned many air shows. Photographers begged for a chance to take her picture. Bessie's face appeared in many newspapers and magazines. Bessie loved to pose for the camera, and she loved every minute on the field, almost as much as being in the sky.

Bessie Coleman and an unidentified friend

An important air show in Wharton, Texas, brought Bessie there to perform. One of the attractions was a scheduled parachute jump. Parachute jumping was novel and popular. A girl had agreed to make the jump, but the show started and the girl hadn't appeared. People waited and became impatient. Soon they demanded refunds. Bessie made the jump herself and saved the show.

Miriam A. "Ma" Ferguson, Texas's governor, made her headquarters in Austin, Texas. She, too, admired Bessie very much. She invited Bessie to her home and entertained her as she would a head of state. Bessie enjoyed the love and respect of both whites and blacks.

All the while, Bessie performed in air shows and held fast to her dream of opening the flying school. More women began taking flying lessons now, but Bessie saw that blacks did not come to the air fields and shows. If she didn't open the school soon, many young African Americans might never have a chance to get above the cotton fields and into the sky. When Bessie made up her mind, nothing could stop her. She said, "The sky is the only place where there is no prejudice, the only place to be free."

Money, lots of money, would be needed to open the flying school. People anxious to see Bessie in person and hear her lecture, flocked to colleges and universities, flying schools, churches, town halls, and auditoriums. Bessie loved to speak to groups about how she realized her goal of flying. She inspired many people, not only those of her own race, but white people as well. Audiences listened, spellbound. Bessie wanted people to know that it was possible to overcome prejudice and poverty. She wanted them to know that if she could accomplish her dream, they could do the same.

Bessie told everyone she met about her plans for the flying school. She tried to convince wealthy blacks that her cause was important. She tried to get them to contribute to the fund for the school. This didn't happen, but Bessie wasn't discouraged. She continued to save her own earnings.

Bessie conducted air shows all over the country. During the winter months, she left the Midwest and traveled to the

Bessie's Curtiss JN-4

Pacific and Atlantic coasts. The warm climates of California and Florida encouraged aviation.

California was noted for its air races. Bessie entered an air race from San Diego to Long Beach, a distance of about 150 miles. Bessie got lost in the dark. To make matters worse, she found herself without lights. She made it through and landed in an open field not far from Long Beach.

In 1924, the Ford Motor Car Company produced the ten millionth car. America was on wheels and wheels needed tires. A tire company located in California offered Bessie a contract. They wanted her to advertise for them. Bessie was excited and honored. This gave her a wonderful opportunity to earn money for the flying school. She went to Santa Monica and signed the contract.

Not many hotels in Santa Monica would rent a room to a black. Bessie stayed at the Young Women's Christian Association and enjoyed an evening meal at a diner. The local movie house was showing a silent film, Charlie Chaplin in *The Kid*. Bessie walked two blocks to the theater and enjoyed the show. But she wished Hollywood would produce movies about flying.

The morning Bessie scheduled to test the company's plane, the sun shone brightly, the balmy weather promised to hold. Bessie was impressed with the up-to-date air field. She breathed in deeply, enjoying the good smell of gasoline, castor oil, doping, and canvas. Safety features were everywhere.

Planes that were well repaired or clean made Bessie feel first class.

Bessie climbed aboard the plane and took off. The motor purred, the plane responded to her every command as if she and the plane were one. Suddenly, Bessie realized something had gone terribly wrong. The engine, though it tried desperately to fire correctly, weakened and then came back. Then the engine grew silent. She heard only the wind whistling against the wing wires before the plane took a dive to earth.

Chapter 7

Bessie awoke to the clean antiseptic smell of St. Catherine's hospital in Santa Monica. She looked up, hoping to see blue skies and clouds, but saw instead a stark ceiling.

She lay in a white bed, conscious of pain in every part of her body. Her hands and arms, covered with bandages, felt numb. Somewhere in the shadows a nurse moved about on silent feet.

Bessie floated off, sleeping, dreaming of a shiny new red plane that soared above the earth, and she controlled the machine with skill and daring. Again she opened her eyes. A doctor stood beside her, searched her face, and looked into her eyes. Then he jotted notes on a chart. When he finished, he tucked the chart under one arm and smiled.

"Bessie?" he said softly.

Bessie tried to rouse herself, to raise her body, to sit up, but she could only fall back against the pillow. She had to fight to keep her eyes open.

"Bessie Coleman. Hmmmm. I've heard about you." The doctor continued to smile. "Seems to me you're somewhat of a fallen angel. You fell out of the sky yesterday and needed to be put back together."

Bessie blinked. The doctor examined the chart again, then tucked it back under his arm. "You broke several ribs . . . a leg, and . . . you have many cuts and bruises. We patched you up. You'll be as good as new, but it will take time."

Bessie wanted to ask how long it would be before she could fly again, but her eyes closed before she could say a word and she fell asleep.

Walter arrived the next day to find a crew of reporters hovering around Bessie's bed. One of the men asked, "What shall we tell your fans, Bessie?"

Bessie gave a faint salute with a bandaged hand and said, "Tell the world . . . I'm coming back."

The days that followed demanded another kind of courage

from Bessie. It would be a long time before she was able to fly again.

The hospital released Bessie after a few weeks, but the doctor suggested she take time out to rest and recuperate. Bessie went back to Chicago and rented a small apartment. She needed time to relax, to think, and to heal.

Bessie spent a whole year alone in her apartment. She redecorated the place, she collected every book on aviation she could find, and she read and studied. But Bessie's heart belonged to flying. She couldn't stay out of the sky for very long. Soon she began making daily flights at a nearby airfield. She had to stay in practice, though it would be a while before she went back to a full schedule of air shows.

Every day Bessie received letters from important people who asked to visit. Everyone admired her spirit, her courage, and her ability. One day she received a letter from Prince Kojo, whose family ruled on the Ivory Coast of Africa. He explained that he would be in Chicago on business and would like to meet with Bessie. She was excited and flattered. Of course she wanted to visit with him. When the day of his arrival came, she was nervous. She had dusted her oak furniture many times. She plumped the cushions on the blue settee again and again. Things had to look special for a prince.

The meeting with Prince Kojo became one of the most exciting events of Bessie's life. She was so glad she had taken French lessons and learned the language. Prince Kojo spoke French, but not English. He had been educated in France.

During Bessie's year of rest, she made additional plans for the flying school. She knew she must return to performing in air shows. The money she had saved was nearly gone, and she needed funds for the flying school. Her reputation had not suffered in any way because of her absence from the air scene. People had not forgotten her; they welcomed her back. She found herself just as popular as before. Brave Bessie had come back!

Bessie often said the sky was the only place where people could be free, where prejudice was unknown, where everyone was equal. This may have been another important reason why she felt compelled to fly, a reason why she wanted to "come back!" Come back she did, and she picked up where she had left off. She went back to barnstorming.

Bessie's sister, Elois, had married and now lived in Georgia. Bessie, scheduled to fly at Orlando, Florida, in the spring of 1926, decided she had to see Elois first. Just before Christmas, Bessie took the train to Georgia and brought gifts for Elois and her family.

What a grand reunion the sisters had. They talked about their childhood, about Mama, the family, about Waxahachie. This year the Christmas tree had electric lights, not candles. Elois owned a wonderful Victrola and records, even records with Christmas music. A crank on the side of the cabinet had to be wound periodically, but the sounds delighted everyone. They interrupted the stories about growing up and their memories now and then with holiday treats, cookies, cake, candy, and popcorn. Together, the sisters cooked a dinner just like Mama used to make.

The splendid holiday went all too fast. It was soon time for Bessie to leave. Goodbyes were difficult. Bessie and Elois had tears in their eyes at parting. Bessie hugged Elois as if she would never let her go. Bessie's path in life, far different from her sister's and the rest of the family, called to her and she obeyed.

Chapter 8

$\mathcal{A}$ir shows continued to be popular. Bessie enjoyed the support and loyalty her fans brought. People loved Bessie, and Bessie loved to entertain. The idle periods between shows gave Bessie the time she needed to campaign for her flying school.

Bessie visited pool rooms, settlement houses, ice cream parlors, fairs, any place where young blacks gathered. She spoke passionately about flying, and her spirit and enthusiasm inspired many. Determined to help members of her race break into aeronautics and contribute their skills, she continued to spend much energy planning for the flying school. In her thrifty way, she kept saving money.

Bessie wrote to Elois often. In one letter she wrote, "I am

right on the threshold of opening a school." Closer now to her goal than ever before, Bessie was elated. Blacks would not have to go to Europe to learn to fly. They could be taught here in their own country, the United States, and Bessie would make it possible.

In the spring of 1926, President Calvin Coolidge lived in the White House, college students swallowed live goldfish for attention, and people danced to the latest dance step, the Fox Trot. Some women bobbed their hair, wore T-strap shoes, short skirts, danced the shimmy, smoked and drank. This was

shocking behavior. These women, freed from restrictive rules and conventions, were called "flappers."

During this exciting period, Bessie went to Florida. She had promised to perform for the Jacksonville Negro Welfare League's annual celebration. The event would honor Bessie. She was particularly excited about this air show because influential African Americans planned to attend. These people, Bessie's own people, had money, enough money to help her establish the flying school for her race.

Progress in aviation had continued to move forward. Newspapers eagerly printed stories about advances in flying. Bessie was thrilled when she read about Richard E. Byrd and Floyd Bennett, who flew from Spitsbergen (Svalbard) to the North Pole and back. In order to investigate the possibility of long-distance flying, Alan Cobham flew

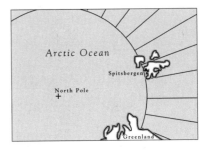

from Croydon, England, to the North Pole and then back to England.

Air shows were still extremely popular in 1926. Americans loved their new talking picture shows, too. People flocked to see Hollywood's handsome actor, Rudolph Valentino, in *The Sheik.* Jazz recordings began to appear, Sigmund Romberg wrote the popular "Desert Song," and A.A. Milne wrote the children's classic, *Winnie the Pooh.*

The air field in Jacksonville the morning of the Bessie's show looked spectacular. The scene resembled a fair, complete with a Ferris wheel, hot dog and lemonade stands, balloons, and music. Bessie could hardly wait to perform her difficult stunts in the sky.

This important air event brought many reporters who hoped to get pictures of Bessie and news of her exhibition. Bessie enjoyed this kind of attention. She dressed in her usual military type clothing for which she had become famous. The morning of the show, Bessie, flushed and excited, and in the company of two companions, decided to have breakfast at the field cafeteria. The restaurant smelled of fried bacon and fresh coffee. A Victrola, nestled in one corner of the room, played "Show Me The Way To Go Home," a popular song at that time. When the machine wound down, a man in a white apron cranked the handle, and the music started up again.

Bessie and her friends chose a table by a window, but, as Bessie passed a group of people already seated, to her surprise she recognized a familiar face. There sat Mr. Abbott, her old friend, the man who had helped her get her start in flying. Delighted to see him, she kissed him on both cheeks. She had learned this greeting in France. Seeing Mr. Abbott was almost like seeing a member of her family. Mr. Abbott's happy expression told Bessie how glad he was to see her, too.

Bessie introduced Mr. Abbott to her friends. "This is the man," she said, "who gave me my chance. I shall never forget him."

Mr. Abbott and Bessie chatted about flying, the newspaper business, and the old days at the White Sox Barber Shop. Then she told him about her trial flight, scheduled later that day. Mr. Abbott pursed his lips and lines gathered on his forehead. He told Bessie not to take the plane up. Perhaps it was a premonition, he said, but he felt she should not make the flight. He told Bessie that he didn't like the looks of her partner, William Wills, a newly acquired mechanic. Wills had flown Bessie's airplane from Dallas, Texas, to Jacksonville, Florida, the week before. He had been forced to land twice because of engine trouble. Bessie had great faith in Wills, and her usual optimism told her everything would be fine.

William Wills, piloting the plane, took off with Bessie and climbed to 3,000 feet. The crowd watched, never taking their eyes away from Bessie's plane. After ten minutes in the air, it became apparent that something had gone wrong. The craft suddenly nose-dived and sped downward to earth. At 2,000 feet the plane flipped over, and Bessie fell to her death. For some unknown reason, Bessie had not worn a parachute, an unusual mistake. She had always been very careful about her safety.

William Wills remained with the plane and died instantly when it crashed. Bessie's plane burned when a spectator threw a lighted cigarette and ignited gasoline that had spilled at the crash scene.

Later, when the accident was investigated, a wrench was discovered, jammed between the plane's gears.

Bessie Coleman's life ended on April 30, 1926. Instead of the wonderful fair that had been planned in Bessie's honor, hundreds of people came to say goodbye to Brave Bessie. She was buried in Lincoln Cemetery in Chicago.

The *Chicago Defender* later wrote, "Though with the crashing of the plane, life ceased for Bessie Coleman, enough members of the race had been inspired by her courage to carry on in the field of aviation, and that whatever is accomplished by members of the race in aviation will stand as a memorial to Miss Coleman."

In the next few years, exciting and spectacular events in aviation followed. Charles A. Lindbergh, in May of 1927, crossed the Atlantic Ocean nonstop. Mildred Doran, on August 16, 1927, became the first American woman to attempt a solo ocean crossing. She died crossing the Pacific Ocean, an experienced pilot who never even got her pilot's license.

Charles A. Lindbergh and Commandant Harvey A. Burwell beside Lindbergh's Spirit of St. Louis, Bolling Field, Washington, D.C.

Bessie's dream of opening the flying school for people of color did not end with her death. William J. Powell, an early black flyer and promoter, organized the Bessie Coleman Club in the early 1930s. In 1932, Powell made Bessie's dream come true. He said, "Because of Bessie Coleman . . . we have overcome the barriers within ourselves and have dared to dream. Today there are many black aviators, men and women, and there are schools to teach them how to fly." During the Depression era he urged young people of color to "carve out their own destiny in a transportation system free of racial discrimination."

Later, in 1937, Amelia Earhart, whose daring and courage pushed her to the limits of possibility, lost her life in an attempt to fly around the world. When asked the question, "Why do women fly?" Amelia answered, ". . . to fly is to flee."

Amelia Earhart

After Bessie's death, another young African American woman, Willa B. Brown, gained special notice in the aviation field. In 1939 she led the fight for men of color to be included in the Army Air Corps. She established the first privately owned black flying school in the United States, and it was approved by the government. This school trained the men who became pilots in the 99th Pursuit Squadron, a highly decorated black flight squadron of World War II.

Marge Brown, a famous barnstormer said, "Women are seeking freedom. Freedom in the skies. They are soaring above the temperamental tendencies of their sex that have kept them earthbound. Flying is a symbol of freedom of limitations."

Bessie's words, "The sky is the only place where there is no prejudice. Up there, everyone is equal. Everyone is free," remind us that flying allowed people to shed the bonds of poverty and prejudice. On the anniversary of Bessie's death, each year black pilots drop flowers over her grave. As a pioneer in aviation, she will never be forgotten. Her bravery and determination made it possible for her to overcome the barriers of poverty, race, and gender, to fly. She inspired many people who came after because she dared to dream.

Bessie paved the way for today's African Americans to realize whatever dreams they might have, especially the desire to fly. Bessie continues to inspire people of all races. The sky is the limit!

$\mathcal{P}$ostscript

Bessie's relatives and many organizations have worked tirelessly to see Bessie's picture appear on a United States postage stamp. In April 1995, the United States Postal Service issued this thirty-two-cent stamp. This honor gave Bessie Coleman the place in history she deserves.

Books about Airplanes

Ault, Phil. *By the Seat of the Pants*. Dodd, Mead & Co., New York. 1978

Becker, Beril. *Dreams and Realities of the Conquest of the Skies*. Atheneum, New York. 1967

Boyne, Walter J. *The Aircraft Treasure of Silver Hill*. Rawson Associates, New York. 1982

Brown, Fern G. *Amelia Takes Off*. Albert Whitman & Co. Morton Grove, Illinois. 1985

Gilbert, James. *The Great Planes*. Grossett & Dunlap, Inc., Publishers, New York. 1970

Gill, Brendan. *Lindbergh Alone*. Harcourt Brace Jovanovich, New York. 1977

Gunston, Bill. *The Encyclopedia of World Air Power*. Crescent Books, New York. 1980

Ingoglia, Gina. *Big Book of Real Airplanes*. Putnam, New York. 1987

Mann, Peggy. *Amelia Earhart: First Lady of Flight*. Coward McMann, Inc., New York. 1970

Ogden, Bob. *Aircraft Collections of the World*. W.H. Smith, Publishers, New York. 1986

Peterson, David. *Airplanes*. Children's Press, Chicago. 1981

Smith, Elizabeth Simpson. *Women in Aviation*. Walker & Company, New York. 1981

GLOSSARY

Ace. A fighting pilot who brought down five or more enemy aircraft.

Aerodrome. Field where airplanes land and where they are kept.

Barrel. Rolling the airplane over and over in the air.

Biplane. Airplane with two sets of wings, an upper and lower.

Controls. The stick and rudder used by the pilot to control the plane, all positions of wings and nose.

Dope. A cellulose acetate to shrink and strengthen cloth surfaces of the airplane.

Fuselage. The body of the airplane.

Immelmann. A half-roll on top of a half-loop.

Joystick. The airplane's steering and control lever.

Rib. A fore-and-aft portion of the wing. It gives the part of the wing its form and transfers the load from skin to spars.

Roll. A maneuver in which airplanes make complete rotations, ending with the plane flying in the same direction in which it started.

Sauce. Gasoline or petrol.

Spar. A round metal or wood piece that supports rigging. Any member of the main longitudinal member of an air plane wing.

Wing strut. A brace that connects the upper and lower wings of a biplane. It runs from the base of the fuselage diagonally up to the wing.

Zoom. The plane is pitched suddenly upward at great speed. This is usually accomplished after a dive has given the craft greater momentum or power.

ILLUSTRATIONS COURTESY OF

frontispiece National Air and Space Museum, Smithsonian
Institution, Photo No. 84-14782

Page 8 National Air and Space Museum, Smithsonian
Institution, Photo No. 94-9641

Page 14 Collection of New-York Historical Society

Page 22 National Air and Space Museum, Smithsonian
Institution, Photo No. 85-11029

Page 22 National Air and Space Museum, Smithsonian
Institution, Photo No. 92-14959

Page 23 National Air and Space Museum, Smithsonian
Institution, Photo No. 94-9640

Page 26 Ellis County Museum, Inc., Waxahachie, Texas

Page 40 National Air and Space Museum, Smithsonian
Institution, Photo No. 93-7758

Page 40 Arthur W. Freeman (Bessie Coleman's nephew)

Page 41 Arthur W. Freeman (Bessie Coleman's nephew)

Page 48 National Air and Space Museum, Smithsonian
Institution, Photo No. 87-10381

Page 48   National Air and Space Museum, Smithsonian
            Institution, Photo No. 82-3644

Page 53   Arthur W. Freeman (Bessie Coleman's nephew)

Page 55   National Air and Space Museum, Smithsonian
            Institution, Photo No. 94-9642

Page 69   History of Aviation Collection, University of
            Texas at Dallas

Page 70   History of Aviation Collection, University of
            Texas at Dallas

Page 71   Arthur W. Freeman (Bessie Coleman's nephew)

Page 73   United States Postal Service

Come Josephine in My Flying Machine

Chorus

Come Josephine in my Flying Machine,

Going up she goes! Up she goes!

Balance yourself like a bird on a beam,

In the air she goes, there she goes!

Up, up, a little bit higher,

Oh! my! the moon is on fire,

Come, Josephine in my Flying Machine,

Going up, all on, "Goodbye!"

INDEX

— A —

Abbott, Robert Sengstacke, 33–35, 44, 66–67
Africa, 32, 60
America's Sweetheart. See Pickford, Mary
Anthony Fokker's Aircraft Company, 38
Army Air Corps, 70
Atlanta, Texas, 8
Austin, Texas, 53
Avord, France, 36–37

— B —

barnstorming, 46–49, 61
    photographs of, 48
Bat Boat, 21
beaucoup bon, 37
Bennett, Floyd, 65
Benz motored L.F.G. plane. See L.F.G. plane
Berlin, 42
Bessie Coleman Club, 69
biplane, 38, 76, 77
Brown, Marge, 70–71
Brown, Willa B., 70
Bryan, Alfred, 24, 81
Byrd, Richard E., 65

— C —

California, 55–60
Camel, 22
    photograph of, 22
Chaplin, Charlie, 56
Checkerboard Aerodrome, 44
Cherokee, 10–11
Chicago Defender, 33, 44, 68
Chicago, Illinois, 27, 29–35, 41, 44, 60, 68
chili parlor, 41
Cobham, Alan, 65

Coleman, Bessie
   accidents, 57–60, 67–68
   air shows, 7–9, 43–49, 52–54, 55, 63, 64–68
   barnstorming career, 46–49, 61, 63–68
   birth, 10
   childhood in Waxahachie, 10–20, 23–27
   church activities, 15–16
   contract with tire company, 56
   death, 67–68
   education, 12–15, 23–27
   flight training in France and Europe, 36–42
   formation of the Bessie Coleman Club, 69–70
   learning French, 35
   living in Chicago, Illinois, 29–35, 41, 60–61
   meeting Prince Kojo, 60–61
   parachute jumping, 53
   photographs of, 6, 40, 53, 71
   picking cotton, 11, 13–14, 17
   plans for flying school, 49–50, 54–55, 61, 63–65
   postage stamp, 73
   reading, 14–15, 19–20
   receiving her pilot's license, 40–41
   working as manicurist, 32–35
   working in chili parlor, 41
Coleman, Elois, 11, 13, 14, 17, 18, 20, 25, 27, 62, 63–64
Coleman, George, 10–11, 19
Coleman, Georgia, 11, 12, 18, 25, 27, 44–45
Coleman, John, 27, 43
Coleman, Nilus, 11, 12, 18, 25, 27
Coleman, Susan, 11, 12, 13, 14, 15, 18, 50–51
   photograph of, 41
Coleman, Walter, 27, 43, 59
Come Josephine In My Flying Machine, 24, 81
cotton industry, 17
   photograph of, 13
Coolidge, Calvin, 62
Croydon, England, 65
Curtiss, 7, 8–9, 44, 45, 47
   photographs of, 8, 55
Curtiss Field, 7, 44
Curtiss, Glenn, 8

— D —

Dallas, Texas, 10, 67
Delineator, 19
Desert Song, 65

Doran, Mildred, 69

— E —

Earhart, Amelia, 48, 70
    photograph of, 70
England, 65

— F —

Ferguson, Miriam A. "Ma," 53–54
Fitzgerald, F. Scott, 34
Five Civilized Tribes, 11
flappers, 64
Florida, 55, 62, 64, 67
    map of, 64
Flyer, 19
Fokker Triplane, 23
    photograph of, 22
Fokker, Anthony, 23, 40
Ford Motor Car Company, 29, 56
Ford, Henry, 29
Fox Trot, 64
France, 34–42, 61

— G —

Germany, 23, 40, 42

— H —

hand organ, 16
Hemingway, Ernest, 34
Houston, Texas, 46, 49, 51

— I —

Immelmann, 44, 76
Ivory Coast, 60

— J —

Jacksonville Negro Welfare League, 64
Jacksonville, Florida, 64, 65, 67
Jenny. *See* Curtiss
JN-4D. *See* Curtiss

— K —

Kid, The, 56

— L —

L.F.G. plane, 42
Langston Industrial College, 26
Langston University. See Langston Industrial College
Le Crotoy, 37–40
Lincoln Cemetery, 68
Lindbergh, Charles A., 48, 69
    photograph of, 69
Long Beach, California, 55–56
Long Island, New York, 7

— M —

Midway Airport. See Checkerboard Aerodrome
Milne, A.A., 65
Missionary Baptist Church, 15–16
Model T Fords, 29
monoplane, 38
Mr. Wilson's General Store, 18

— N —

New York Times, 43
Nineteenth Amendment, 31–32
Ninety-ninth Pursuit Squadron, 70
North Pole, 65

— O —

Oklahoma, 10, 11, 26
    map of, 26
Orlando, Florida, 62

— P —

Paris, France, 34, 36, 48
penguin, 37–38
Pickford, Mary, 36
Powell, William J., 69–70
Prince Kojo, 60–61
Pup, 22

— R —

Red Baron. *See* Von Richthofen, Manfred.
Red Cross, 21, 36
Richthofen glide, 44
roller, 38
Romberg, Sigmund, 65

— S —

San Diego, California, 55
Santa Monica, California, 56–60
SE5A, 22
Sheik, The, 65
Show Me The Way To Go Home, 66
Sopwith, Tommy, 21–22
SPAD, 23
    photograph of, 23
Spitsbergen (Svalbard), 65
    map of, 65
SS *Noordam*, 43
St. Catherine's Hospital, 58–60
Staaken, 42
Stinson, Katherine, 49
suffragettes, 31–32
Sunday School, 15

— T —

Texas, 10, 46, 49, 52, 53–54, 67
    map of, 10
Tin Lizzies. *See* Model T Fords
Topsy. *See* Uncle Tom's Cabin
Tour de Piste, 38
triplane, 22, 23, 38

Tubman, Harriet, 15

— U —

Uncle Tom's Cabin, 15
    illustration of, 14

— V —

Valentino, Rudolph, 65
Victrola, 62, 66
vin ordinaire, 37
Von Richthofen, Manfred, 23, 44

— W —

Washington, Booker T., 15
Waxahachie, Texas, 10, 11, 20, 26, 27, 51, 52, 62
    photographs of, 13, 26
Wharton, Texas, 53
White Sox Barber Shop, 32, 67
Wills, William, 67–68
Wilson, Woodrow, 36
wing walkers, 48
Winnie the Pooh, 65
World War I, 21, 23, 39, 40
World War II, 70
Wright, Wilbur and Orville, 10, 19

— Y —

Young Women's Christian Association, 56